Alfred's Premier Piano Course

Dennis Alexander • Gayle Kowalchyk • E. L. Lancaster • Victoria McArthur • Martha Mier

Alfred's *Premier Piano Course* Performance Book 4 includes motivational music in a variety of styles, reinforcing concepts introduced in the Lesson Book 4.

The pieces in this book correlate page by page with the materials in Lesson Book 4. They should be assigned according to the instructions in the upper right corner of selected pages of this book. They also may be assigned as review material at any time after the student has passed the designated Lesson Book page.

A compact disc recording is included with this book. It can serve as a *performance* model or as a *practice* companion. See information about the CD on page 32. A General MIDI disk (30204) is available separately.

Performance skills and musical understanding are enhanced through *Premier Performer* suggestions. Students will enjoy performing these pieces for family and friends in a formal recital or on special occasions. See the List of Compositions on page 32.

Edited by Morton Manus

Cover Design by Ted Engelbart
Interior Design by Tom Gerou
Illustrations by Jimmy Holder
Music Engraving by Linda Lusk

ISBN-10: 0-7390-5148-2
ISBN-13: 978-0-7390-5148-1

Letters from Home

CD 1/2 GM 1

Premier Performer

Listen for the perfect balance between the hands by playing the LH softer than the RH melody.

Lesson Book: pages 8–9

Tarantella Siciliano

CD 3/4 GM 2

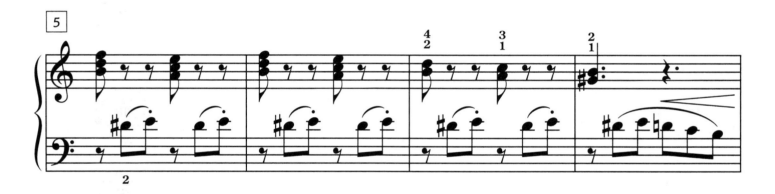

* Indicates a clef change for the RH.

Premier Performer

Create a change of mood in measures 17–38 by carefully following the dynamics.

A Winter's Tale

CD 5/6 GM 3

Premier Performer *Create a different mood at measure 17 by playing this section a little faster. Return to the original tempo at measure 29.*

Cappuccino Boogie

CD 7/8 GM 4

Driving, with energy

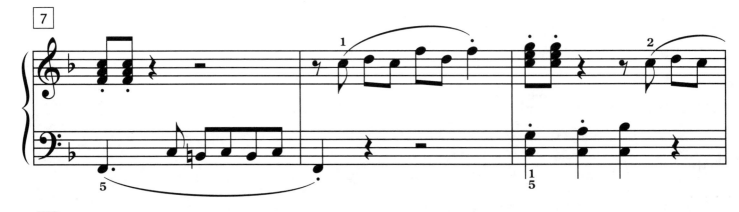

Premier Performer

For a different style, play at a slower tempo and swing the eighth notes.

Spring
from *The Four Seasons*

CD 9/10 GM 5

Antonio Vivaldi

> **Antonio Vivaldi** (1678–1741) was a noted Italian composer and violinist. Earlier in his life, he became a priest. His nickname was "the red priest" because of his red hair. His most famous piece was The Four Seasons, a set of four violin concerti. Each concerto is dedicated to a season of the year. Spring is possibly the most popular, and was also known to have been a favorite of King Louis XV of France.

Premier Performer   *Imagine different instruments of the orchestra as you play with a steady, march-like tempo.*

Along the River Seine*

CD 11/12 GM 6

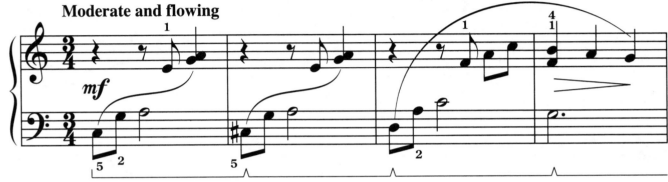

* The Seine is a river in northwestern France that runs through the city of Paris.

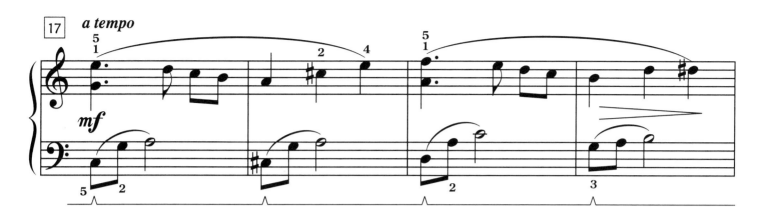

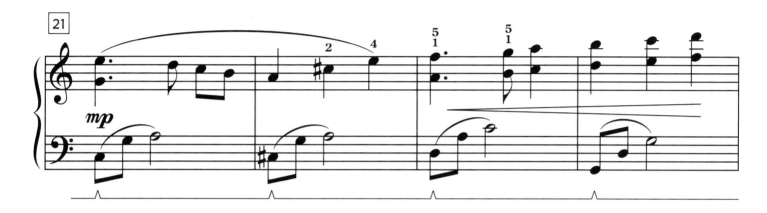

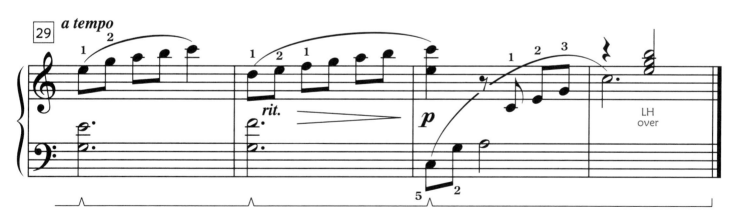

✦ Premier Performer — *As the melody flows between the hands in measures 1–8, smoothly connect the notes as if they were being played by one hand.*

House of the Rising Sun

CD 13/14 GM 7

Traditional

* Continue changing the pedal on beat 1 of each measure.

Premier Performer *Listen for smooth, connected pedal changes.*

Spanish Guitars

CD 15/16 GM 8

Lesson Book: page 29

The Legend of Atlantis*

CD 17/18 GM 9

Moderate and flowing

* According to legend, Atlantis is a continent that sank into the Atlantic Ocean and will someday rise again.

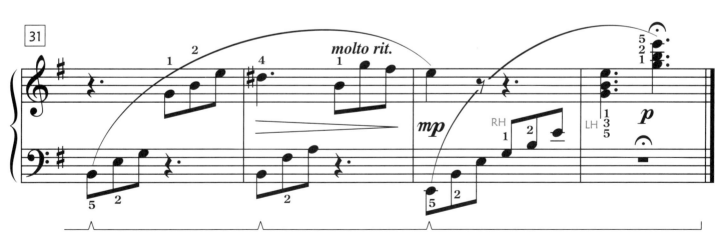

Premier Performer

Let the melody line flow smoothly and evenly between the hands.

Red Rock Rag*

CD 19/20 GM 10

Happily, but not too fast

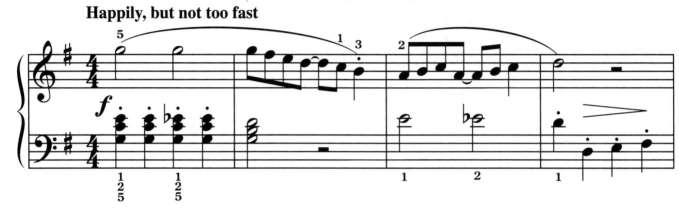

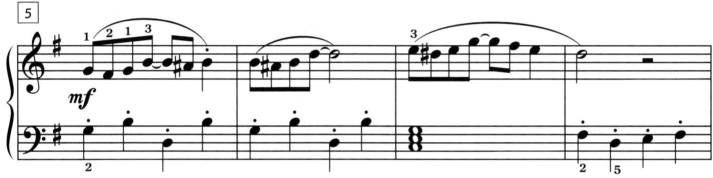

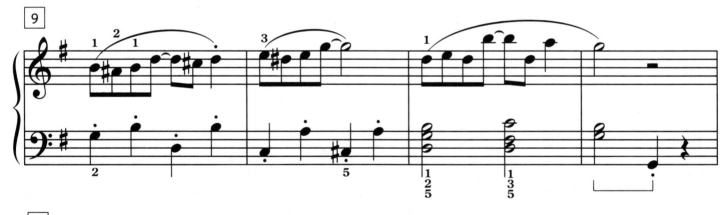

* Red Rock Canyon is located in the Mojave Desert, a few miles west of Las Vegas, Nevada.

Premier Performer *Play with a steady beat and even eighth notes.*

Old-Time Movie

CD 21/22 GM 11

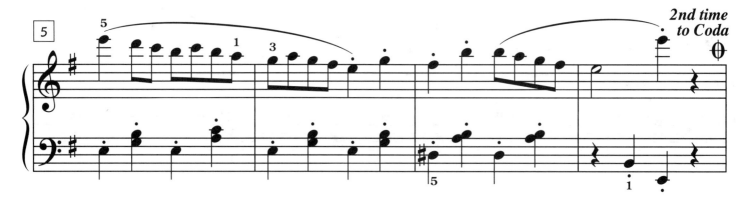

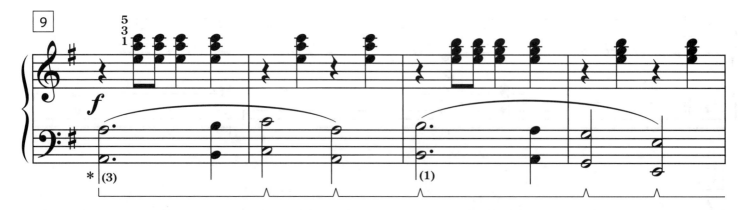

* Students with small hands may omit the top notes of the octaves and use the fingering in parentheses.

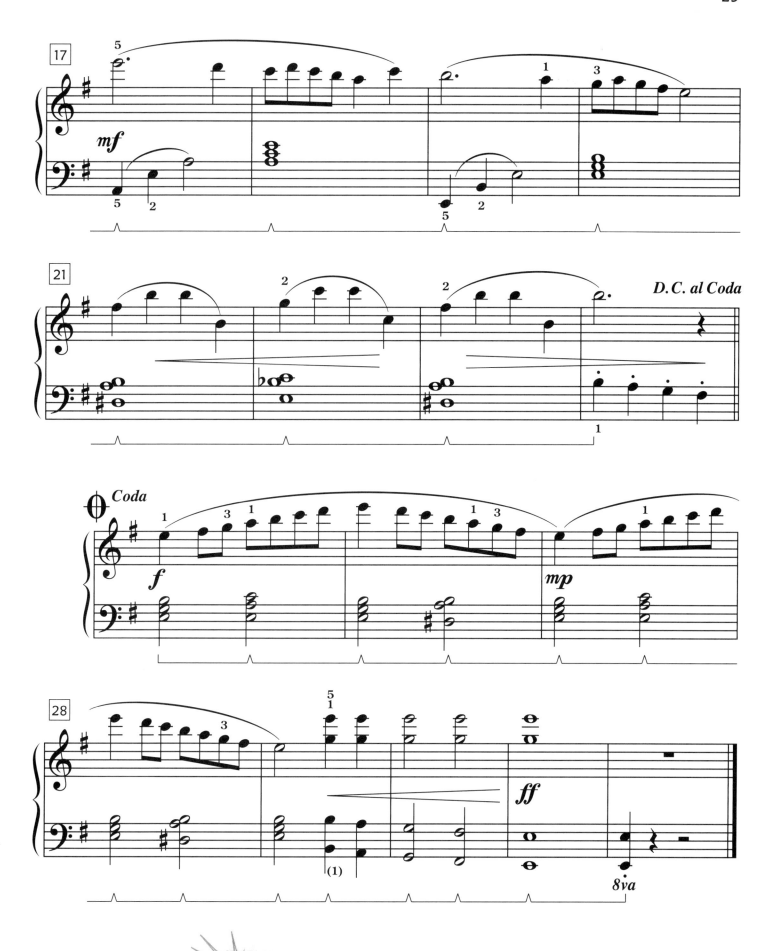

🌟 **Premier Performer**   *Bring out the LH melody in measures 9–16.*

Lesson Book: page 35

Rhythm Workout

On your lap, tap the rhythm 3 times daily as you count aloud.

Sonatina in C Major

CD 23/24 GM 12

William Duncombe
(18th century)

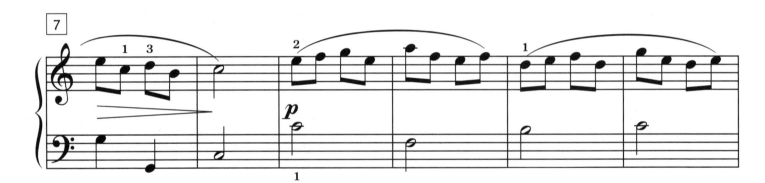

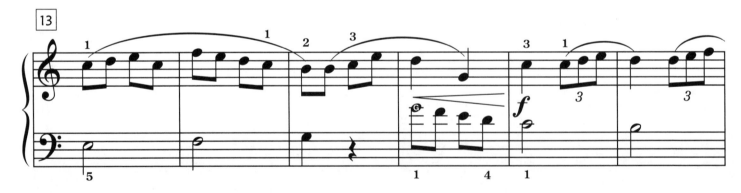

Premier Performer *Count the triplets and eighth notes carefully to keep the tempo steady.*

Lesson Book: pages 36–37

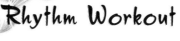

Rhythm Workout

On your lap, tap the rhythm 3 times daily
as you count aloud.

Minuet in F Major

CD 25/26 GM 13

Wolfgang Amadeus Mozart (1756–1791)
K. 2

Allegretto

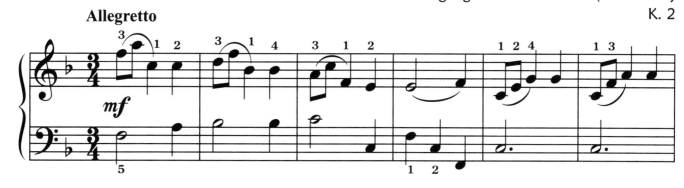

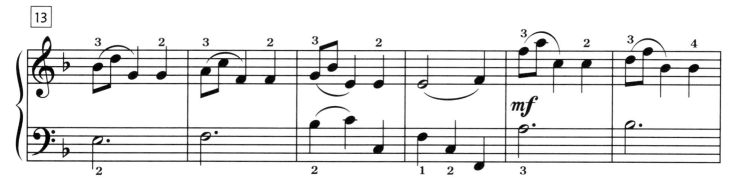

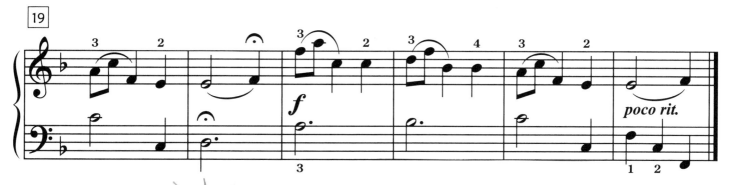

Premier Performer

A minuet *is an elegant dance in* 3/4 *meter.*
Play with a strong first beat in each measure.

The Steeplechase*

CD 27/28 GM 14

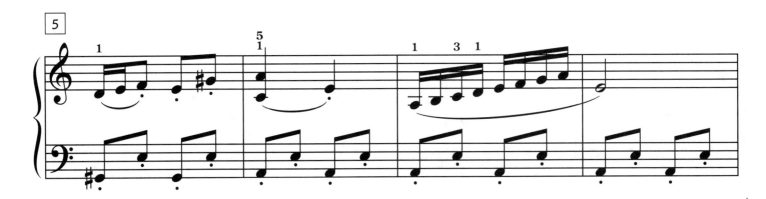

* A *steeplechase* is a horse race that includes jumping obstacles.

Premier Performer *Use a rounded hand position and firm fingertips to play all sixteenth notes evenly.*

Lesson Book: pages 42–43

Musette in D Major

from the *Notebook for*
Anna Magdalena Bach

CD 29/30 GM 15

The ***Notebook for Anna Magdalena Bach*** *was a gift from J. S. Bach to his second wife and mother of 13 of his children. The notebook had the initials "A. M. B." and the year "1725" in gold on the cover. It is not known how many of the pieces included in the collection were actually composed by Bach himself. Many of the family's favorite pieces were copied in the handwriting of Bach, Anna Magdalena and some of the younger family members.*

Johann Sebastian Bach (1685–1750)*
BWV Anhang 126

* Although this piece is included in J. S. Bach's *Notebook for Anna Magdalena Bach*,
 historians doubt that he actually wrote it.

Premier Performer

Keep the tempo steady without stopping between measures 2–3, 4–5, 6–7 and similar places.

Lesson Book: pages 44–47

Premier Toccatina*

CD 31/32 GM 16

Rhythm Workout

On your lap, tap the rhythm 3 times daily
as you count aloud.

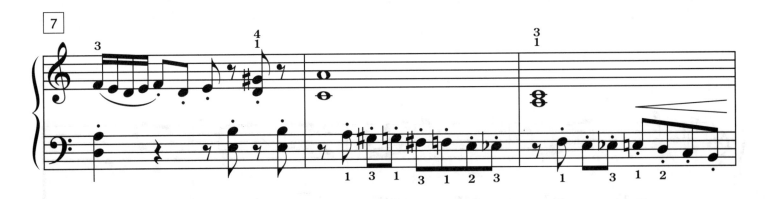

* A *toccatina* is a short *toccata* (display piece).

Premier Performer

Observe all dynamics and articulations (staccatos, slurs and accents) to create an exciting mood and character.

List of Compositions

Note: *Each selection on the CD is performed twice. The first track number is a performance tempo. The second track number is a slower practice tempo.*

The publisher hereby grants the purchaser of this book permission to download the enclosed CD to an MP3 or digital player (such as an Apple iPod®) for personal practice and performance.

CD Performances by Scott Price